FOREVER SUMMER

A Legacy of Eternal and Heavenly Strength

KEITH ETHRIDGE

LAKEVIEW
PUBLICATIONS

Info about bulk orders or public speaking events:
Spudjr33@yahoo.com

Contents

"I have told you these things, so that in me you may have peace. In this world you will have tribulation. But take heart! I have overcome the world."

John 16:33

To my beautiful wife Kristy, thank you for your consistency in the way you love. No matter the storm, you Love unconditionally. Thank you for your example and obedience to God. Thank you for loving our family the way you do! Thank you for recognizing and understanding how we are all "wired" and loving us, anyway. Most of all, thank you for your unwavering support on this journey and the way you love me!

To my precious Summertime, thank you for your example of willingness to be obedient to God while you were here with us. A daddy couldn't be any prouder of his daughter. I will miss you every second until we are reunited!

FOREVER SUMMER

A Legacy of Eternal and Heavenly Strength

KEITH ETHRIDGE

LAKEVIEW
PUBLICATIONS

Introduction

Have you ever felt lost, alone, and questioning God's purpose?

We all face trials that can feel overwhelming. We question, we doubt, and we wonder, "Why, God, why?" But within these challenges lies an opportunity for growth and spiritual renewal.

One of the greatest challenges I have ever faced began with this question. Through prayer, meditation, and the systematic unpacking and rebuilding of my faith through that challenge, I found myself channeling my grief through this journey of pain, to the pages you now hold in your hand. As I began to tell the story you are about to read, I was asked by my publisher, "Who is this book for?"

When I first pondered the question, "Who is this

book for?" my heart immediately replied, "Me." This book is a personal journey, inspired by God's grace, to guide me through life's wilderness. As I delved deeper into His word and experienced His transformative power, I yearned to share these revelations with others.

"This book is for me, isn't it?" I looked at the pages in my hand, and the story God had let me be a part of, and the answer became clearer than ever before. Dear reader, this story is for "Us."

This book is for all who wander in the wilderness, feeling lost, helpless, and questioning God's purpose. Together, let's discover the path to hope, healing, and divine guidance. It's for those who have cried out to God, asking, "Why?" It's for all of us who seek understanding, hope, and a renewed purpose.

I pray that you will allow some part of my journey through this storm to encourage you to stay in the fight and be a warrior just like my daughter.

Keith

ONE

Every Summer Has A Story

Summertime is what I called my daughter – Her name is Summer Rae Ethridge. I always thought that no one has ever had a more perfect name to reflect their personality.

Summer Rae was a ray of sunshine, illuminating every room with her infectious laughter and quick wit. Her passion was a flame that burned brightly, fueling her relentless pursuit of her dreams. She was a force of nature, unstoppable in her determination to overcome any obstacle that dared to stand in her way.

While she was not very big in stature, there was no denying that she was every bit a warrior. She was way too pretty to be that tough! Summer's looks would fool you until you got to know her…which usually didn't take long! She had high expectations for herself and expected the same from others. She was unafraid to "call it like she saw it".

Summer was drawn to the "cowboy life" or "ranch life" as she got older and I never really understood why, since I never owned a horse or a cow in my life…then I started to meet the people! These people lined up exactly with Summer's personality in their passion, expectations, undeterred resilience, and warrior spirit. Obstacles like hard work or long hours are a way of life for these folks. It was easy to see why Summer was so drawn to this lifestyle. Summers co-workers and friends were truly like family to her, and I will always be grateful for the way they supported and looked after my girl.

Summer and I always shared a love of the outdoors. It was clear at an early age when she would always want to come hunting or fishing with me – she just loved being in nature.

I'll never forget when she took her first deer, she lit up like a Christmas tree – man she was excited! She loved the whole process from me rubbing the blood on her cheeks to cleaning the deer! I can still hear her saying, more like yelling, I got him Deddy!! I smoked him!!

We shared a lot of fun times in the outdoors; hunting and fishing that I will cherish forever. It was so much more for me, and I think she realized that the older she got. As she got older and had more responsibilities, she would make time to schedule a Sunday afternoon hunt with me and she would want to sit together instead of going to different stands.

She made a point of going with me and my dad to a college football game that I know she had no interest in; we always had a great time. She always made time for the people in her life that she loved. She always wanted to be a part of their lives in whatever these people and her had in common, shopping, hunting, fishing, ranching, sports…whatever it was, she was in!

There was a time I remember when she was in college at East Central and working. We weren't spending much time together, and that would not work for Summer. I will never forget her phone call to me, it went something like this.

"Deddy! We bout to start walking every morning at the dam!" It wasn't a question – it was a statement.

I laughed and said, "Summertime I usually leave the house about 6-6:15 going to work."

Her response was "They got lights at the dam."

Over the next few months, me, Summer and her dog Si met at the dam at 5am. I wouldn't take anything for those early morning walks. Obstacles were a challenge to Summer, but she was determined to overcome them. She refused to let anything, no matter how small, create distance between us.

I could go on and on about my Summertime and how special she was and all the things she taught me by the way she lived her life. She was a beautiful, big-hearted, passionate, kind, spitfire warrior who would not back down. There is no telling how many stray cats and dogs she "saved" in her 23 years…lol…that determined spirit can have a downside! From a very early age, it was her mission to save every stray animal she saw, and some that were not strays! I can remember several times riding down the road, Summer would blurt out, "Deddy! We need to go get that dog; he is lost!"

I would respond with, "Summer, that dog is in some one's yard, it has a collar on."

She would usually respond with something like "Well, I will be watching him."

When she got old enough to drive…you can only imagine!!

All of Summer's character traits served her well in her 23 years here – but make no mistake about it – her strength was in Christ. Summer was unashamed about her faith in God and as I would soon find out, He is the ONLY way!

TWO

Summer's Heart

These walks at the lake were so special because looking back, I can see how God used this time for Summer and I to talk about so many important things that at the time, I didn't even realize she was dealing with.

These early morning walks with Summer and Si were a gift, a precious opportunity for one-on-one time. In the quiet solitude of the pre-dawn hours, we shared moments that felt both timeless and fleeting. It's a difficult thought to process, isn't it? To be so present in the moment, yet to know that time itself is slipping away.

I could listen to things she was dealing with in her life that I would have never known about had we not been "walking". I was able to hear how she processed and dealt with life problems in a way that our normal relationship would not have allowed. She would open up to me very honestly about her personal relationships, her ideas about career options, her relationship with God, it was a time looking back that I was able to see exactly how special she was beyond just a father's love for his daughter. I can remember being so proud of her and amazed by her maturity at such a young age.

Around this time, Summer had ended a long-time relationship with a young man. Our whole family loved this young man and still do to this day. He is a fine young man with a fine family, and I know he loved Summer and all of us. Summer was heartbroken over it, and we talked about it several times on our walks. She explained to me she loved him, but she knew she didn't love him like she needed to for it to be forever. I remember her crying as she talked through how it wasn't fair to him to "lead him on" about their future. I remember her talking about how unfair life was and questioning whether she should just not say anything because she loved him, and everybody loved him, and it was so hard, and a flood of tears came with the realization that she had to be honest with him and herself. I stood there hugging her while she/we cried. In that moment of vulnerability, I was able to explain to her that sometimes "true love" is letting go. I look back and know that God was preparing me even then for things to come. God was giving me words of power that He would bring to my own heart and mind as I wrestled with the steps that lay ahead on my own journey of faith. I am still amazed at Summer's maturity level at such a young age. I am also extremely comforted to know that while neither of us knew what was down the road in our lives, God did and the image in my mind of a father holding his child in the stillness of that morning, has comforted me in my own steps of faith. My heavenly father was holding me on that quiet morning as well, and He allowed me to see the desire of a father to comfort and love his child so I could better feel His love when I would need it the most.

During that time, Summer was working for our local veterinarian in the small town we live in. Her love for animals had always attracted her to one day becoming a vet. Tyson, the local vet, had agreed to hire Summer to work part time around her school schedule. This turned out to be another God thing. The people at this vet clinic made such an impression on Summer. She talked about them constantly – and believe me – that girl could talk! She learned so much from working with this group. The animal/medical/pet care she learned pales compared to what she learned about life. She would tell me stories about people a lot more than stories about animals. She would talk about how this staff would handle situations with people - both good people and sometimes not so good people - with a level of compassion and caring that was hard for Summer to understand.

Although she loved everyone there, Tyson was her favorite! I learned a lot about Tyson through Summer's stories, and I will always be thankful that God brought them into each other's lives. He was always honest with Summer…even when it wasn't what she wanted to hear; he told her anyway. She respected him for his honesty and his work ethic, both of which he instilled in her. Summer looked up to Tyson and I appreciate the example he set for her. I know he loved Summer as well. I know because I see it in his eyes. Tyson has a son about the age of one of my grandsons and I see him from time to time at the baseball field. He comes to shake my hand every time, when we make eye contact, I see it. Every time I see it.

Thank you, Tyson for investing in and loving my daughter like one of your own.

This time at the vet clinic would also lead Summer to another realization – she didn't want to be a vet. I remember her struggling with this for a long time. She would talk about the things she loved about it and the things she didn't. She was struggling and I remember her looking to me for an answer. I remember talking about this on many "walks" and I wanted her to make this decision, not me. Summer was always a deep thinker, and she always prayed a lot about whatever she was dealing with. I remember encouraging her to not rush the decision and to remember that hard decisions are typically difficult ones. I remember telling her about how all our decisions have consequences and that she has the responsibility to make the decisions for her path in life. I encouraged her to wait for God. It's not complicated, but it's not easy!

Summer ended up following her heart and deciding her path was not down the road to vet school. She ended up with a Bachelor's degree in animal and dairy science with a concentration in livestock production and management from MSU and absolutely loved where that path was leading her. We have all heard it said that if you find something you love for a career that you will never "work" a day in your life.

Well, Summer found it!

Summer went to "work" a lot, but it truly wasn't work for her. She absolutely loved her "job", all the people and especially Johnny. Johnny was her horse; he seemed kind of wild to me with a hard head and a mind of his own…kind of like Summer. It's probably why she loved him so much? She would often tell me about his "attitude" but that he was so smart. Again, Summer in a nutshell – lol.

Summer worked at PLI in West Point, MS. She seemed to fit in perfectly there. I can only imagine what those guys thought when they first saw Summer, all 120lbs of her. What she lacked in size, she made up for in attitude and confidence. I met and talked to a few of the men she worked with and heard many stories about all of them. These are salt of the earth, hardworking guys, and girls that are unimpressed with what you say, they form their opinions on what you do. Summer became like a daughter/sister to many of these people. She earned their respect based off her word and work ethic. Several of these guys talked to me about her "spit-fire" personality and willingness to learn, and they would always comment on her work ethic.

I had the pleasure of meeting a very large man from that industry at the hospital in Tupelo. This giant of a man shook my hand with tears in his eyes and handed over a very generous check to Summer's family that in his words was "not a gift, this was earned". He had sold a cow at auction and this cow would be bought and sold again many times, one after another, by different ranchers and cattle owners, then be returned to the original owner. All this money was given to Summer's family on her behalf. Summer was one of their own and they take care of their own. I will never forget these people and the impact they had on my daughter. God always took care of my girl and He used her to impact many people for His kingdom while she was here.

The pain of losing a child will never diminish – but the hope we have in God won't either. One of Summer's favorite verses of scripture, which is highlighted in her bible, is John 16:33 – beside this verse of scripture she wrote the words: He is Hope – what a powerful verse description! Jesus provided a way for us to be reunited again; through His sacrifice we have hope! It's not complicated, but it's not easy!

"I have told you these things, so that in me you may have peace. In this world you will have tribulation. But take heart! I have overcome the world."

John 16:33

THREE

Tupelo

Friday, June 30, 2023 – Turning into the office on this Friday morning was the same as any other day, except it was Friday. Friday's are always a little different, a little better if you will. Maybe it's just knowing you can "unplug" for a couple of days and just do what you want to do. For me that typically involves family, golf, hunting or fishing, depending on the time of year.

This particular Friday I had been thinking about the upcoming 4th of July Holiday. My wife and I had been talking about having family over like we had done in the past. Fireworks with grandchildren, food, family etc. All those thoughts quickly went away as I turned into the parking lot.

My phone rang and my life forever changed.

I will do my best to walk you through the next 12 days. Even now, over a year later, it's hard to separate days, probably because it was so painful and emotional.

I wheeled around in the parking lot and called my wife Kristy. I told her about Summer being in an accident and being airlifted to Tupelo. I hurried home to pick her up, and we took off to the hospital in Tupelo.

We arrived at the hospital that day at the same time as Summer's mom and her husband and they would only let Summers's mom and myself go to where Summer was initially. I felt the panicked feeling as we approached the room and my knees almost buckling when I saw her. I saw the dried blood and all the machines and the medical staff. I remember her boots and bloody clothes on the table by the wall and most of all I remember the helpless feeling and a loud ringing in my head.

Eventually, the medical staff asked us to go up to the ICU waiting room and they would come to update us. I still have dreams, regularly, about that waiting room, the sounds, the smells, the lonely, helpless feeling. I wondered if this is what prison would feel like. In a way, it was like a prison, but I couldn't stand the thought of not being there. I couldn't stand the thought of going to a hotel or going home even though I hated everything about that place.

That ICU waiting room, and those long hours spent

praying, begging, hoping, making deals, crying out, questioning and even cursing God is where God began to reveal things to me in a way that only God can. The first night in that waiting room, I felt like I was going to have a heart attack. My head was ringing so loud I could barely think. I felt sad and angry and confused and wondering why…why… why!!!

The next day was no different. I remember all the sweet friends and family offering condolences and saying everything was going to be okay and everything that people said would just infuriate me! I hid it the best I could, but I was so angry and nothing anybody said ever helped at all. I just wanted my Summertime back, and I wasn't interested in any other outcome!

My Brother-in-law, Dr. Bill Boren, is a pastor and very gifted man of God that has helped me more than I can begin to express. Bill told me something on that second day after that long night of wrestling with God that I will never forget. He said, "Keith, I want you to know something. Summer will be healed…either in heaven with her Savior or here with us, but she will be healed."

That statement shook me to my core…there was no way to argue, no way to be angry, no disputing this truth. I've heard it said "God might not be on time, but, He's never late!" To me, this is exactly what that means… God's timing is always perfect. The statement from Bill was exactly what I needed to hear, exactly when I needed to hear it. God is good!

That same day, Mandy Stewart brought Summer's bible to the waiting room- another God send for the upcoming night. We were told Summer's bible was found unscathed, sitting on the back seat of her car... where everything else in the car was strewn around and some things unfound. I really don't know what I would have done on that second night if I hadn't had Summer's bible. That bible was like a big bear hug from my Summertime! I didn't want that night to end. I sat up just reading all her comments in the margins and highlighted scriptures that meant so much to her. It was like she was there with me, and I am forever thankful for God's mercy in that time. I have prayed about whether to include this letter I wrote to Summer that night in her bible, but it is part of what happened, and I hope that my journey in this might help someone else come to know the power of our living God.

"But He said to me: My grace is sufficient for you for My power is made perfect in weakness."

2 Cor. 12:9

Saturday, July 1st, 2023 – North MS Medical Center

My Sweet Summertime – I have been praying for you as hard as I possibly can and asking God – very selfishly – for more time here with you. I realize that when I ask and trust God to heal you that I have to be prepared for His will to be done. I just can't imagine having to continue in this old world without you, but the truth is that you were God's before you were my little girl.

Whatever God's plan is for you the truth is- you will be healed!! I am praying that God's plan is for you to be healed here with me and all the people that love you so much. I have been sitting here tonight reading your bible and all your little notes and underlined scriptures and it is truly like you are here with me.

One of my favorite scriptures is Jeremiah

33:3 – I have underlined it in your bible. I pray God will show you things like He has shown me – always ask Him and trust Him!! I truly believe that God is not finished using you to do His work. I pray that he will see fit to give your selfish daddy more time with his sweet Summertime.

You are one of the strongest most determined beautiful people I have ever seen, and I couldn't be prouder of you! God could have chosen to take you at that intersection that Friday morning – but he didn't!

I am holding tight to that and praying and believing that he is going to restore you to whatever it is that he wants you to be, to do his work here.

You are a fighter – You were created by God with a true fighting spirit, and He has equipped you with everything you need to fulfill His plan for you! I will continue to pray for my girl and I will always love you more than I could ever tell you.

I love you forever,
Deddy

"The grass withers, the flower fades, but the word of our God stands forever."

Isaiah 40:8

FOUR

Days of Summer

The next few days following the accident run together in my mind. There were countless visitors and well-wishers, family, friends, and people I didn't know, all with the same message…" Everything is going to be okay."

Was it? Life would be ok for them, but what about us? Was life going to be ok for us?

We were all on a roller coaster of emotions, all of us…praying, begging for some encouraging news from a doctor. I remember hearing things like brain bruise, brain bleed, brain swelling and drains. We looked at computer images of Summer's brain and explanations of what was going on and how they would deal with this or that. There was literally a wall of medicines that Summer was getting, that were supposed to be helping.

At some point, I remember hearing a doctor say something about starting the "wake up process." Looking back, I believe that part of God's mercy was running these days together in my mind. I'm glad I can't remember every day, minute by minute or every conversation we had with doctors. I mostly remember a complete feeling of helplessness.

When I think back on this moment in our lives, I recall a quote that has resonated with me: "God works most powerfully when we feel most powerless." It's in those moments of utter helplessness, when we've exhausted all our own resources, that we're truly open to God's intervention.

We were helpless, but this is where God does his best work!

It's not complicated…but it's not easy!

This "wrestling" with God for me was in its very early stages…this anger I felt by different comments from various well-wishers was also in its very early stages.

There was a prayer vigil planned for Summer in the parking lot at the hospital in Tupelo. There must have been a couple hundred people show up and there were beautiful words spoken and prayers said in honor of Summer and for our family. I am very grateful for every prayer and every person that took not only their time to pray but come to the hospital on behalf of Summer and/or our family. I saw our community come together and support our family in an unbelievable way – there is no way to start thanking individuals because there were countless acts of kindness; many of which I probably don't even know about.

Even in the midst of all this outpouring of kindness, love, and well-wishes…I was pissed! I just wanted everyone to leave, shut up and just go away! This anger was starting to show itself to me more and more and I can remember embracing this feeling. It sounds crazy now, even to myself, as I write this on paper…but it is true. How could this be happening to me, to my family, to my daughter and why!! Looking back, from where I am now, I honestly believe this was the devil trying to get a foothold…and I was listening!

How could God allow this??

The verses of scripture offered as comfort felt like mockery. The promise that "all things work together for the good of those who love God" seemed hollow. Where was this promised good for Summer? Where was it for us? Summer loved God; I loved God. She pursued God's gifts in her life. How could this accident be part of His plan? Where was the good in this?

It wasn't good for Summer. It wasn't good for her family. But could it be that in the midst of this terrible tragedy, God could work something beautiful? Could He use this to bring Him glory? Could He deepen our understanding of His love through this pain and ultimately work all of this for good?

As I write these pages now, I can clearly see that God was at work.

Back in the waiting room, it was the same as it had been. Long hours of helplessness, followed by more of the same. We were all completely exhausted, but not wanting to leave.

There was a doctor, talking with us and sharing his faith. I remember feeling a calm, soothing honesty in his voice that was very powerful. He talked with us, asking about family, other children etc., and had many kind words. The thing I remember most was his genuine concern and his tear-filled eyes – his heart was breaking for us.

He said "I think we have it backwards…we should cry when babies are born and celebrate when people go to be with our Father."

I have thought about his statement many times. Sin in this world causes many storms…Summer's favorite scripture. John 16:33 gives us hope!

> "I have told you these things, so that in me you may have peace. In this world you will have tribulation. But take heart! I have overcome the world."
>
> John 16:33

It's not complicated...but it's not easy!

Thank You, Father, for giving us hope. Through this hope and You making a way on the cross, this sinful world holds no actual power over us. Bring on the storms, because You have the final say...the battle is already over, You win!

One of God's biggest blessings, not only during this time, but of my life, for me, is my wife, Kristy. During this time in Tupelo, when I could barely think, much less function – she was absolutely incredible. We had two other daughters still at home...two and a half hours away from Tupelo and a dad (that would be me) that wouldn't leave the hospital. I am still amazed at how Kristy kept it all together. I don't know how many trips she made back and forth, but I never remember feeling like she wasn't there for me or the girls...it doesn't add up. She is an amazing woman, wife, mother, and friend. The most beautiful person, both inside and out, that I've ever seen or known. Her calmness and inviting demeanor, along with her ability to truly listen, and hear people, are gifts. I'm always amazed at how people want to open up to her. Honestly, it aggravates me sometimes but she just laughs at me and always tries to talk to whoever it is through whatever it is. She is an amazing person and I don't know what I did to deserve her, but I don't know what I'd do without her.

God also used my brothers significantly during this challenging time. Though not biologically related, Alex, Eric, and Michael are as much family as any blood brother. We've been through thick and thin together, and I'm increasingly grateful for their presence in my life. Looking back, I realize they sensed my struggles on a deeper level than I may have acknowledged at the time. I will never be able to thank them enough or repay them enough for all their kindness…not just the days and nights spent with me in that waiting room or the meals or hotel rooms provided for my family or the prayers, phone calls, texts…you name it, they provided it. It was more than all of that. It's hard to put into words, but they knew…they all knew and I know they knew. They were right there with me through it all…hurting, praying and supporting, and still are to this day. They are my brothers and I love them all very much.

Summer was also blessed with many sisters…both biological and non-biological. The "sisters" I am speaking of here are a group of very close-knit friends that grew up together, and like me and my "brothers", I think of them all as "sisters". One afternoon, these friends of summers converged on the waiting room and changed the whole "vibe." Everything suddenly lightened up in that waiting room. There was laughter and talking – hugs and crying…it was like a breath of fresh air with all these young ladies in the room. I remember a time where I was just sitting and watching them interact with members of our family and each other and for a time it was like everything was normal again. These girls were making things for Summer to put in her hospital room with her and telling stories and reminiscing about times and adventures they had shared with Summer. They were so positive and happy, and I was so thankful that God has blessed them all with each other.

This same group of beautiful young ladies met on the anniversary of Summers' passing and had photos taken with a picture of our Summertime. They personally delivered the beautifully framed photos to us, and I wouldn't take anything for them. I hope and pray that these young ladies will always know how much they mean to our family. There is no doubt in my mind that they all know how much they all meant to Summertime.

There is no way this this story would be complete without talking about Summers relationship with her sister Karli. Karli and Summer met when Kristy and I met. They were both 3 years old and only about a month apart in age. Two very different personalities and looking back now its amazing how God knew how much they needed each other! These two very different little girls would learn more from each other than anyone could imagine. The bond these two would develop in their twenty years together is truly incredible. As different as they have always been they always made time for each others issues no matter what. They were both fiercely protective of each other and without fail were always there for each other. I truly believe that God used both of them in each others lives in a very special way to make them who He wanted them to be. I take great comfort in knowing that Karli will always have a very special angel watching over her. They shared a connection that we should all share with our siblings!

W

M

July 9, 2023 is the day God took my precious Summer Rae to be with him in glory. Our two daughters, still living at home with us, Allie and Kyndal, were with us at the hospital, so we had stayed at a hotel that night.

The morning of Sunday, July 9th, we were in a hurry to get up and get dressed to get back to the hospital when my phone rang. I was sitting at the desk in that hotel room listening to the Doctor as his voice cracked and his heart was breaking as he told me she was gone. It is very hard to write about that morning in that hotel room as I sat there listening to the Doctor, and even now, I struggle to find words to describe the feeling. That news is something that every parent hopes they never have to hear and when you do hear it, I'm not sure it is possible to process. The empty feeling of complete hopelessness and loss is indescribable.

Looking back, I see God's grace in that my wife and daughters were all there, we were all together in that moment able to at least have each other. Sometimes all you can do is cry and there is nothing left to say, nothing left to pray – this was that time and that's what we did.

Our precious Summertime was gone. The reality of what my brother-in-law had told me a few days prior had come to be. "She will be healed, either here with us or in heaven with Jesus…but she will be healed."

The feeling of numbness and disbelief were

surreal…almost like a dream. We just sat there for a time and sobbed. In the moment, all I could think about was I needed to get it together and get to the hospital and call my dad, my brothers, my sisters, my family, my brother-in-law…all these people needed to know and I didn't know what to do or how to do it.

The next 3 days were much different. They had to flush all the meds from Summer's organs before they would be viable. This was a very difficult time because we now know God's will but we could still visit with Summer and talk to her and hold her hand just as we had been doing, but it was different. I spent hours and hours thinking about what my life would be like going forward without Summer.

I was reflecting on another tough time just a few years earlier when my son Jake was in a terrible auto accident and was airlifted to Tuscaloosa. Gods plan for Jake was much different. Jake finally recovered, and is now married to his beautiful wife, Avery. I prayed and begged and made deals with God when Jake was in the hospital, just like I did with Summer.

Why were my prayers not answered this time?

The passage that Summer loved so dearly always answers that question now.

"I have told you these things, so that in me you may have peace. In this world you will have tribulation. But take heart! I have overcome the world."

John 16:33

"Likewise, the spirit helps us in our weakness, for we do not know what to pray for as we ought but the spirit himself intercedes for us with groanings too deep for words."

Romans 8:26

I know that one day all my questions will be answered. I know that God's ways are not like ours and I've also learned that we must learn to trust God even when our situation or circumstances don't make any sense to us.

It's not complicated…but it's not easy.

FIVE

Summer's Joy

The next part of our time at the hospital in Tupelo is very difficult for me to think about, so I will do my best to be honest without offending or being overly critical.

I'll start by saying that this would be difficult in any circumstance for the parents of a child. Summer had elected to be an organ donor at the DMV when she renewed her driver's license. I was aware of this decision because it had come up before in conversation. This is a very selfless decision and one that we fully intended to honor.

This was Summer's decision and her wish. She loved the thought of someone getting life changing news and having their prayers answered because of a decision she made. This is a beautiful act of kindness, and I am beyond proud of her for choosing to do this. The problem I had was with how this agency, or more specifically the people who worked for this agency, went about this process.

There were two people from the agency that we dealt with. I will refer to them as miss and mister. I have replayed the events of this time I think of as "organ donation" hundred if not thousands of times in my head, trying to understand why they would go about this process the way they did. I have considered everything from maybe they were understaffed and overworked to maybe it was "company policy." Maybe they had done this so many times they had lost their compassion for the families involved in this process. Maybe to them the donor is just that, a donor, not a daughter.

The first meeting we had with this agency was conducted by Miss when she summoned us to the ICU break room of all places and told us that based on Summer's choice at the DMV to be an organ donor, she would be transported to the agency's facility in Jackson, MS where a more comprehensive harvest could be done. This meeting took place *before* July 9th when it was determined that Summer would not come back to us. To say I didn't respond well to her "telling" us how this was going to go would be a vast understatement. Let's just say this was a very short meeting. After I told her she might want to wait until after Summer had been pronounced deceased…I told her they would not be taking her anywhere and that WE would decide what was going to be "harvested" and where. The anger I was talking about earlier was to a point was hyperventilating and my heart was beating out of my chest.

I took a break and stepped into the hallway outside the waiting room and felt a rage like I had never felt before. At that moment, I am convinced that God intervened on my behalf. I can still see this man in my head. He had on a blue polo shirt with Auburn Baptist Church embroidered on the chest. He walked right up to me and said, "You look troubled, can I pray with you?" I still have chills when I think about this. He prayed with me and asked God to bring me the peace only He can. Then he was gone and I just stood there and cried. My wife, Kristy came out at that time, she was hugging me while I told her of this man, but he was gone. *John 14:18 – I will not leave you comfortless, I will come to you.*

At this point in time, I was so angry at God and buying in to the lies being whispered to me by the devil.

How could God be allowing this? How?

Even in this time of me cursing God and questioning his power, He was faithful to keep his promise to not leave me comfortless. What an awesome God! What a picture of a father with his child.

Suddenly, in my mind, it was me and Summer, and it

was God holding me while I sobbed into his shoulder. It was God, as my father, holding me tight and whispering into my heart, "Keith, sometimes true love is letting go." It was moments like this that happened so many times throughout the process that gave me the strength to move forward. God was giving me His strength in my weakness. As the days would proceed with the organ donor agency representatives, I would need all the strength I could get from Him.

The next meeting with the organ donor agency was in a private conference room where Miss asked if we would listen to Mister on her cell phone if she would call him and put him on speaker. She started by making apologies for him not being there in person, saying something about him having child care issues or something like that. I felt that rage again in my stomach and again, it was another very short meeting. I was shocked and offended he didn't have enough respect to show up in person, much less think I was going to listen to him tell me over the phone what he thought was going to happen going forward. I cut him off and left the room again, completely pissed off and not wanting to deal with them again on any level.

I saw Mister a day or so later in Summer's hospital room and I honestly believe if it hadn't been for my wife and the ICU nurse who insisted he leave immediately, I would have done something very unchristian like. I apologized to the nurse for what I said to him, and she told me I shouldn't apologize, that this was my daughter and all I was doing was protecting her. She told me they could do everything right there at the hospital as far as the organ donation and for me not to worry about it anymore. This nurse was one of the most compassionate people I have ever met, a true angel. That was the last interaction I had with Mister. The remainder of the organ donation was relatively smooth, in my opinion, because of the hospital, not the organ donation agency.

I remember Miss offering updates about finding recipients for Summer's organs and giving us the timeline for when the organ harvesting teams would come. They would take Summer to the O.R. at 2:00a.m. on July 12, 2023. The hospital staff lined the hallway as they took her to the O.R. with all her family and friends walking with her. Their way of honoring her last selfless act. Everyone at North Mississippi Medical Center in Tupelo, MS is top-notch, from the doctors and nurses to the support staff. They could not have been any better to our family and friends throughout our stay with them.

The organ donation agency, on the other hand, presented a different, more challenging experience. They transformed a difficult and emotional process into a gut-wrenching ordeal. I believe I could write an entire book detailing their failures in supporting us and my daughter. It's disheartening to imagine how many families have been mistreated by this duo under the guise of organ donation.

I want to emphasize that my personal experience should not deter anyone from considering organ donation. It's a noble act, and donors are true heroes. I sincerely hope that the agency will implement necessary changes to their staff and treat donors and their families with the respect they deserve.

We left the hospital that night/morning in the darkness, embarking on the longest, saddest drive of my life. The silence in the car was overwhelming, filled with memories, thoughts, questions, funeral planning, and the daunting question of "where do we go from here?" The torrential rain, thunder, and lightning outside mirrored the storm raging within. I remember thanking God for the distraction, even as I resented the need to be grateful in such a painful moment. Little did I know, anger would soon become a formidable opponent.

The details of the day of Summer's funeral are impossible to recount. I will start by thanking First Baptist Church of Collinsville for so graciously allowing us to use this beautiful sanctuary for Summer's funeral. This church and the people stepped up unbelievably during this time for our family. The support from this body of believers was incredible. Many local churches in our area were represented in supporting and loving on our family through this. Churches are only as good as the people who make them up and we have some great churches in our area.

I'm not sure there is a way to accurately assess the number of people who came through the doors of the church on that day, but it was hard to believe. I wish I could remember the words spoken by the pastors or the songs that were sung but I can't. What I do remember are the heartfelt hugs, hand-shakes, and the tear-filled eyes of countless people who came to love on us and encourage us.

Several people who came through the line told me to "trust God". I was infuriated by them saying this and wanted to confront them. I was thinking, "How in the world can you say that to me, I did trust God and He let me down!" I had often prayed for my children's safety and I trusted God to keep them safe. While they intended to comfort me with their words, I was too raw in my grief, and their words only stirred up within me the reality that I was nowhere near finished wrestling with God. The rest of this day is pretty much a blur, and I just wanted to go home.

After the services, we found our home full of people and food. Several of my wife's best friends, Lisa, Jane, Alicia and Wendie, had been there receiving food and organizing everything. They were a God send. Along with Mandy, Soraya and Michelle, they had all done so much to help during this time. These are some truly remarkable women who love my wife and my family very much. I call these women my wife's "squad." They are blessed to have such a strong support system for each other, and I have watched them support each other without fail through many of life's storms. Words cannot express how grateful we are that they were there for us that day.

I could not help but think during the service that day about how many people my daughter had affected in her time here. People of all ages and all walks of life. God had used her across many cultural lines. Summer had a gift of identifying with people from all walks of life. What a great example she set. Summer was able to learn at an early age that people are people, regardless of their line of work or social status. She could identify with someone based on what was on the inside more than what was on the outside. 1 Samuel 16:7 says "But the Lord said to Samuel, 'Do not judge from his appearance or from his lofty stature, because I have rejected him. God does not see as a mortal, who sees the appearance. The Lord looks into the heart."

Our 16-day nightmare had finally ended. The next chapter proved to be more difficult than this one. I will do my best to walk through some lessons that God has taught me on this journey. My prayer for this project has been first to be obedient to what I feel God has for me and second that God will use something that He has revealed to me to be a blessing for someone else in whatever storm they are in or they might have endured.

It's not complicated…but it's not easy!

"Rejoice in hope; be patient in tribulation; be constant in prayer."

Romans 12:12

SIX

Summer's Song

When the funeral is over and everyone goes back to their normal routine and the reality starts to set in that there is a "new normal", I had to face the glaring question. What do you do now?

This empty sense of a piece of you is missing, forever, is a gut-wrenching feeling. All you have are memories, pictures, texts, and videos of someone who was such a beautiful and important part of your life. Everything that you see or hear seems to remind you of something that leads to another memory. I would go to the store, church, work or absolutely anywhere and someone would inevitably say something that would absolutely infuriate me. All I could think about or focus on was the fact that Summer was not here anymore, and never would be again. I could never see, hear, or hug her ever again. I didn't understand it and I wasn't interested in hearing anyone else's opinion of why or what they thought I should be doing to cope, and I sure wasn't interested in hearing I needed to TRUST GOD! In my mind, I had "been there, done that" and had the scars in my soul to show it.

I remember a guy telling me one day that "God must have needed her more than she needed to be here." I've never been accused of being able to hide my expressions very well, according to my wife, and if that's true, I'm sure this fellow realized I wasn't very fond of his statement. I just shook my head and walked away.

There were many other instances that people would say things that I didn't understand or even people who would see my wife and me together and completely disregard her and only address me with their condolences about Summer. Even though my wife would always handle this with grace and class, I knew it hurt her feelings and it would enrage me. Summer and Kristy shared a deep, loving bond, a bond as strong as any mother and daughter could have. This is a fact known by all who knew them.

My bother-in-law Bill checked on me from time to time and warned me about the grieving process and how it affected people differently and how I needed to be patient. He would ask me questions about things and send me books and material to help me process these feelings I was having. Bill has never made me feel pressured to talk or made me feel guilty about what I told him. He has always made me feel like I could reach out to him at any time and I have on many occasions. I remember one conversation where I was telling him I didn't feel like I was managing all this very well. He let me talk for a while and when I was finished, he said something like, "Keith, this is not something you can manage. You are not at work." Bill has a God given talent for hitting you with truth and there is no way to argue. He has taught me so much by saying so little. Bill told me that It was okay to be angry with God and "wrestle" with God. He always backed up what he was telling me with scripture; it's hard to argue with scripture or Bill. Bill is a sharp dude!

When I started this writing project, one thing I prayed for was that God would use this to help someone who was grieving for something in their life. To do that, I felt like I need to be as transparent as possible, even if it reflects poorly on me. I pray that in the end, God will get all the glory for what He has revealed to me, for where He has brought me, and for where He has planned for me to be.

> "For I know the plans I have for you," declares the Lord, "plans to prosper you and not to harm you, plans to give you hope and a future."
>
> Jeremiah 29:11

I have mentioned previously that things would anger or infuriate me. This had become more and more prevalent as time passed. In the weeks and months after the funeral, I had immersed myself in books and articles about how to handle grief. I can remember my wife commenting on how much I was reading and I remember that making me mad! I was on a mission to make sense of something that makes no sense. Isaiah 55:8 was a tough one for me to accept.

> "For my thoughts are not your thoughts, neither are your ways my ways," declares the Lord."
>
> Isaiah 55:8

I felt like God owed me an explanation for what He allowed to happen to my daughter, and I thought I could figure it out. There had to be a reason.

Why?

This question was burning in me and building more and more anger the more I searched for an answer that did not exist. My constant searching was causing problems at home that I didn't care to see, much less deal with.

I had become withdrawn from my wife and children and was completely consumed with my search for answers. All the while this anger continued to build in me because I couldn't make it make sense. I would sit in my office at work, consumed by thoughts and questions about why this happened. I would be driving and be totally consumed by this, watching TV, cutting grass, taking a shower, anything, and everything I did was consumed by these thoughts and questions about why!

I embraced the anger that was building in me, and to think about this now seems crazy, but it is true. I remember feeling okay with being mad. I remember thinking that I had a right to be mad and to hell with everything and everybody! All this anger that I was bottling up eventually had to blow off. I am ashamed to say that I took out all this pent-up hostility and anger at the person I love the most, my wife Kristy.

She was concerned that I was not myself and withdrawing from our family. Instead of me being able to talk to her about how I was acting, I would explode. I would say terrible, mean things to her often blaming her for how I was acting. I remember telling her that if she didn't like how I was acting, she didn't have to be there and maybe she should just leave. I look back now, and it breaks my heart that I acted the way I did and said the things I said to the person I love most in this world. I look back and can only imagine what my precious daughters must have thought about me and how I was treating their mother not to mention treating them. I wish I could say that this was a one-time occurrence, but it wasn't. It was a cycle of building up anger and blowing up, over and over, all while reading everything I could find about how to handle the grieving process and searching for the answer to a question that didn't exist.

Why?!

As I look back on this difficult time on this journey, I can see where God was at work.

> "What do you think? If a man owns a hundred sheep, and one of them wanders away, will he not leave the ninety-nine on the hills and go to look for the one that wandered off? And if he finds it, truly I tell you, he is happier about that one sheep than about the ninety-nine that did not wander off."
>
> Mathew 18:12-13

I was most definitely a lost sheep, but God kept his promise! I would like to recognize a few Godly men that helped me through this time more than they know. I hesitate to mention these men because I know that they aren't looking for any praise or attention, but I thank them for being obedient to what they believe God calls us as believers in Him to do.

> "Love the Lord your God with all your heart and with all your soul and with all your mind and with all your strength. The second is this: 'Love your neighbor as yourself'. There is no commandment greater than these."
>
> Mark 12:30-31

There is certainly no order of importance to these men as they all invested and continue to invest in me as brothers in Christ. Pastor Dr. Bill Boren, Pastor Daniel Fortenberry, Pastor Caleb Hughes and Mr. Darrell Butler. I am beyond thankful because God used these men in my life to be a light for Him.

> "In the same way, let your light shine before others, that they may see your good deeds and glorify your Father in heaven."
>
> Matthew 5:16

If you are struggling with a storm in your life that seems insurmountable, please don't give up, instead give it to Jesus! That statement "Give it to Jesus" was a huge hurdle for me. I don't know if I'm alone in this, but that statement meant little if anything at all to me during this time. I have heard this statement used my whole life, "Just give it to Jesus or you have to give it to the Lord."

I honestly never put much thought into this statement, probably because I had never been tested in my faith and trust in God like this before. This statement was told to me many times by many people as they offered their condolences about Summer.

If you are in the midst of a storm and are angered or confused by someone telling you to give it to God, I would like to offer what God revealed to me about how to do this. During this time when I was so angry, lost and felt like nothing really mattered. And honestly, I really didn't care. I realized that Summer would have been ashamed of me for the way I was acting. The way I was treating Kristy and the girls would have disappointed her to say the least. It was at this point when I truly began to cry out to God. I fussed at God about the promises he had made about never leaving me and always being there. I would read scripture aloud to God like:

> "So do not fear, for I am with you; do not be dismayed, for I am your God. I will strengthen you and help you; I will uphold you with my righteous right hand."
>
> Isaiah 41:10

"Do you not know? Have you not heard? The Lord is the everlasting God, the Creator of the ends of the earth. He will not grow tired or weary, and his understanding no one can fathom."

Isaiah 40:28

"Trust in the Lord with all our heart and lean not on your own understanding;"

Proverbs 3:5

"Call to me and I will answer you and tell you great and unsearchable things you do not know."

Jeremiah 33:3

and Summers favorite:

"I have told you these things, so that in me you may have peace. In this world you will have tribulation. But take heart! I have overcome the world"

John 16:33

I read in one of the many books or articles, as I was searching for answers about "how to give it to God" where the author was describing God's character traits, things like: Humility, compassion, gentleness, self-control, patience, and obedience. At the end of the article the author asked how many of these qualities do others see in you?!! It was like a slap in the head, and as if God was asking me point blank this question. I just sat there crying and asking God to forgive me for how I had been treating my wife and family. I realized that for me to "give things to God" I needed to be more like Jesus! I was ashamed of myself because I had failed the people that I love most in this world! Of these character traits of Jesus, I couldn't honestly say that I wasn't an example of any of them! NOT ONE!

If you are struggling with giving something to God – maybe you need to do what I had to do. Ask yourself that same question and see how you line up with the character traits of Jesus. I realized that because I had never been tested on this level that I didn't truly understand the words faith and trust. I had been playing games with God because I had never actually had to put these tools to use! I heard a preacher say recently that "Having faith has no power. The object of our faith has power". Proverbs 3:5 says "Trust in the Lord with all your heart and do not lean on our own understanding". I truly believe that unless you have been tested at a certain level, it is very difficult to fully understand the true meaning of these two words – Faith and trust.

Hebrews 11:1 tells us, Faith is the assurance of things hoped for; the conviction or evidence of things not seen. It's easy and nice to talk about these words, but very difficult to actually put them to use. It's not complicated...But it's not easy!

If you have accepted God as your personal Savior, He will never leave you and will always be with you!

> "No one will be able to stand against you all the days of your life. As I was with Moses, so I will be with you; I will never leave you nor forsake you."
>
> Joshua 1:5

If you have not made this decision, I will tell you that there is not a more important decision you have to make! From the time sin entered this world in the Garden of Eden, we have been and always will fight against the devil and his storms. Only through Christ do we have hope! John 16:33 He is Hope! He has made a way.

> "Jesus answered, "I am the way and the truth and the life. No one comes to the Father except through me."
>
> John 14:6

Deciding to follow Jesus is the least complicated, yet most difficult thing there is! Roman 12:2 tells us not to be conformed to this world but be transformed by the renewal of your mind.

I want to challenge you with a question that our preacher hits us with often: what are you going to do with Jesus? God is constant, consistent, and never changing. He desires us and offers ultimate satisfaction in this sinful world, but we have the freedom to choose.

Learning to trust God and his promises, and I mean truthfully trusting when there is nowhere else to turn, is the type of trust I didn't think I would have ever known had this not happened to my daughter. If you are in a situation where you have nothing else, nothing makes sense and you can't find any answers, please don't give up until you have explored the promises that only came from Christ! He will not let you down! He didn't let me down, and I was about as lost and angry as you can imagine.

2 Corinthians 12:9 says, but he said to me; my grace is sufficient for you, for my power is made perfect in weakness. God does some of his best work in us when we are at our worst. When our circumstances and situations become too much for us and we feel like we have nowhere else to turn; God is faithful. This is the level of trust that I'm not sure many people understand or even can understand until they find themselves in these situations. Something else that God has shown me through this journey is how close we all are to the "edge". I think this has to do with having compassion. I am talking about genuine compassion. Jesus-like compassion. Again, this word compassion now has a completely different meaning because of the road I have traveled. I now can understand how someone might do or say things that at one time in my life, might have seemed unbelievable or inconceivable.

I think of it as we are all one phone call from having our lives completely turned upside down, to where nothing else even matters. When we are thrown into this type of tailspin, I don't think we can right the ship without help. I searched for help in books and articles, but I'm sure other people search for answers in other ways, like alcohol or drugs or even consider ending their life. Psalm 34:18 tell us that the Lord is near to the brokenhearted and saves the crushed in spirit. Whatever your circumstances, no matter what you have done or said, it's not too big for God!

If you don't know him, He is waiting, and He is Hope!

Maybe you are someone like me who has been a Christian for a long time but had never been tested like you are now, or maybe you are a new believer, or wherever you are. God is trustworthy and faithful. I know God can do anything. My bible shows me example after example of miraculous, unexplainable things that God has done, but until it is you that needs a miracle or something unexplainable to happen, I think it's impossible to know how you will react.

I have to tell you that if this is you and like me, you have failed miserably in how you handled your circumstances, know that YOU failed because YOU tried to handle it alone! If you try to fight the devil on his turf, YOU WILL LOSE!

EVERYTIME!

We were not designed to fight these battles alone. The devil uses sin to get a foothold, to create doubt. The road of doubt leads to death.

> "There is a way that appears to be right, but in the end, it leads to death."
>
> Proverbs 14:12

Jesus tells us in John 14:6 I am the way the truth and the life. It's not complicated…But it's not easy!!

"Call to me and I will answer you and tell you great and hidden things that you have not known."

Jeremiah 33:3

SEVEN

Summer's Light

I was listening to a sermon recently on a long drive for work. The preacher was talking about how we as human beings are "wired." He said humans are wired to *think feel behave,* in that order.

What we think leads to us feeling a certain way, and that leads to a behavior. He said that believing in what God said, regardless of what you feel, is genuine faith. So, I take that to mean that no matter what you feel, no matter what your "phone call" was or what your circumstances are, no matter what you feel, have real faith, we have to believe what God said to be true! Wow, talk about "it's not easy"!

God has never promised us that following Him would be easy, but He promises us John 16:33 "in me you may have peace, in the world you will have tribulation, but take heart, I have overcome the world". I want to encourage you that the road to Jesus is a unique journey for everyone. It is, most of the time, a process. I know God can do whatever he wants, however he sees fit, but in my experience, this journey to Jesus can take a while. For some of us hard-headed people, a little longer! If you are a long time Christian, please remember what this journey might have looked like for you.

If you are new in the faith or have not yet relented to God's calling, please understand that this is a marathon, not a sprint. There will be storms, some stronger than others, but rest assured, there will be storms. I don't know what you may face and you may think that God could never forgive you for what you may have done. That is one of the devil's biggest lies!

That same preacher I was just talking about said in this same sermon – the problem isn't "you don't know what I've done", the problem is "you don't know what He did". If you don't know what God did, that is the problem. Learn to wait on God! Learn to listen, learn to trust, and learn to have faith. It's okay to mess up but learn through the mess up. God built you; he knows you, he has plans for you! I've heard it said that all that matters is how you finish! I love that, and I believe that! I know that it's true because of Jesus' promise to the criminal hanging on the cross next to Him.

"Assuredly I say to you, today you will be with me in paradise."

Luke 23:43

God longs for us to be with Him in paradise. It is right there, waiting on us. It's not complicated…but it's not easy!

As Christians, we have a responsibility not only to tell people about Jesus and who He is and what He has done, but we also have the responsibility to mentor new Christians. We are called to invest in our brothers and sisters in Christ and to hold each other accountable, as well as to help each other navigate the storms of this life. All too often, we are so concerned about reaching new people for God's kingdom that we forget about mentoring and helping to develop them afterword.

Often, we are content to get someone baptized, and that is the end. Matthew 28:19-20 God tells us to "go and make disciples of all nations, baptizing them in the name of the Father and of the Holy Spirit", but that's not where it ends. In verse 20, God tells us to "teach them to obey everything I have commanded you. And lo, I am with you always, even to the end of the age". We as Christians, need to be honest with ourselves about our commitment to undergird and invest in each other's lives. Let's not be found guilty of "checking boxes" i.e.,

I've been baptized, I go to church, I read my bible, etc. We are called to do something! We are called to be Jesus' hands and feet here on this earth.

> "What does it profit my brethren, if someone says they have faith but does not have works? Can faith save him?"
>
> James 2:14

So many of us are comfortable when we are checking those boxes that we become complacent, weak, and soft Christians. Let's challenge ourselves to "put in the work", be proactive Christians that invest in others and come alongside each other with the characteristics of Jesus.

Joshua 1:8 tells us to meditate day and night on God's word so that we may be careful to do according to ALL that is written. If we are just going to church and reading our bible, is that enough? My bible challenges me to be like Jesus, and when Jesus was on this earth, He was not here to check boxes! He was here to do the will of His father. That example was given because this is exactly what we as Christians are called to do!

My pastor and I had a conversation recently where we discussed this issue, and we ended up talking about the culture in which we live. It's very easy to get comfortable with where we are as Christians because of the freedoms we enjoy as Americans. We are spoiled rotten. We worship when we want, for as long as we want, in plush airconditioned comfort without the threat of anyone or anything stopping us. We are accustomed to immediate gratification in our culture. We don't have to really push ourselves for things which leads to us being lazy! This laziness bleeds over into other parts of our lives, like our Christianity.

We need to approach our Christianity with the same sense of urgency that we approach whatever we consider being the most important thing in our lives. We put way too much emphasis on things that are of no eternal significance.

At the end your time on this earth, what is going to matter?

When you leave here, you are going to one of two places. Heaven – Revelation 21:4 says, "A place where there is no more death, sorrow, crying or pain." Hell – Matthew 25:46 says, "And these will go away into everlasting punishment but the righteous into eternal life."

Have you ever thought about how long "everlasting" or eternal" is? One illustration I heard/saw one time from the pulpit, was the speaker was holding the end of a white rope. The white rope had a piece of black tape around the very tip of the rope. This black tape he told us represented our time here on earth. The rope ran across the stage and into a big cardboard box. The speaker pulled this white rope for a long time from the box as it piled up on the stage. He never got to the other end of the rope and when he finally stopped pulling rope, he said this rope represents eternity.

Now if we know that we have these two choices about where we spend eternity – eternal punishment or eternal life. We need to get busy about being about God's business! We need to get a sense of urgency about things of eternal significance and things that really matter.

I challenge you to take an honest look at where you are currently and where you think God wants you to be. Please don't think of spiritual maturity as being a certain age. I honestly believe that my Summertime was more spiritually mature at the time she met Jesus than I was. I thought I was somewhere that I wasn't.

God can use terrible situations and circumstances to do incredible things in your life, if you let Him. I certainly never would have asked for the circumstances that led me to where I am currently on my journey with Jesus. However, I'm not sure I would have ever gotten here without them!

I encourage you to learn to take on the characteristics of Jesus and watch what He can do in your life. Whatever your path has looked like, whatever you have done or whatever has happened to you is not too big for Jesus! We all have different paths for different reasons. Let God use you and your path to change someone's life.

The bible tells us in psalm 139:16 that God knew our days here before we were created. My Summertime lived the life she was created to live. It was not nearly long enough for her selfish daddy, but it was perfect in her heavenly Fathers plan. God has a plan for your life too, and I encourage you to find out what it is. Your story is incredible! No matter your age in earthly years, God has a purpose! There are many examples of God using people of all ages in the bible to accomplish his plan. Let's not let the blessings that God has poured on us as Americans cause us to be lazy Christians. Let's not settle to live our life, just checking boxes! You're not too old, you're not too young! Let's be obedient and have a sense of urgency for the things of God.

Jesus tells us in Luke 8:5-15, the parable of the sower of the seeds. Some seeds fell by the wayside, some fell on the rock, some fell among the thorns, and some fell on fertile ground. Where do you fall in the choices of these four places?

The seed being the word of God, is everywhere! No matter where you are God is there. It is because of sin that it is so difficult to stay on the good fertile ground all the time, but that doesn't change the fact that God is still there! The devil likes nothing more than to take those seeds that are by the wayside out of our hearts.

LET'S NOT LET GOD'S WORD FALL ON A "ROCK HARD" heart – a heart where we hear Gods word and receive it with joy on Sunday, then we go into the world and quickly fall to the first temptation that comes along. Let's guard against those seeds that fall among the thorns – those that are choked out by the pleasures of life.

God gives us the ability to choose and the choices we make have consequences. Verse 8 tells us that "But others fell on good ground, sprang up, and yielded a crop a hundred-fold." I'm here to tell you that God is always there, and he will not leave you. You may not choose Him, but He is still there! I know because he dragged me back to fertile ground kicking and screaming. I was so mad at God for what He allowed to happen to Summer that I didn't care about anything He had to say about it. I was just angry, and I felt content to stay that way.

I was looking through Summer's bible one day at her notes she had written in the margins, and I came across Luke 8:49-56. Summers interpretation of this scripture is this "Girl, get up!

"While Jesus was still speaking, someone came from the house of Jairus, the synagogue leader. "Your daughter is dead," he said. "Don't bother the teacher anymore." Hearing this, Jesus said to Jairus, "Don't be afraid; just believe, and she will be healed."

When he arrived at the house of Jairus, he did not let anyone go in with him except Peter, John and James, and the child's father and mother. Meanwhile, all the people were wailing and mourning for her. "Stop wailing," Jesus said. "She is not dead but asleep."

They laughed at him, knowing that she was dead. But he took her by the hand and said, "My child, get up!" Her spirit returned, and at once she stood up. Then Jesus told them to give her something to eat. Her parents were astonished, but he ordered them not to tell anyone what had happened."

Luke 8:49-56

There will always be a negative voice!"

God used this interpretation of His word in my life in a huge way! It was like Summer was telling me this!

Get up!

I want to encourage you…Girl/Boy – Get up!

God is waiting, He is there – He will not disappoint! My prayer from the beginning of this writing endeavor has been that God would use this journey of mine to help someone who has lost their way. I'm here as living proof that God is bigger than whatever it is! If you will just trust Him and have faith in Him, much easier said than done, He will give you a peace that defies anything you can imagine! Lord, thank you for Luke 15:4-7!

> "Suppose one of you has a hundred sheep and loses one of them. Doesn't he leave the ninety-nine in the open country and go after the lost sheep until he finds it? And when he finds it, he joyfully puts it on his shoulders and goes home. Then he calls his friends and neighbors together and says, 'Rejoice with me; I have found my lost sheep.' I tell you that in the same way there will be more rejoicing in heaven over one sinner who repents that over ninety-nine righteous persons who do not need to repent.
>
> Luke 15:4-7

Thank you for dragging this lost sheep back to fertile ground! It's not complicated, but it's not easy!

I use that phrase, "It's not complicated, but it's not easy" a lot in this writing. This phrase is something God gave to me in my struggle with Him. I use this often to remind myself-almost daily-as I continue my journey.

I think now, more than ever before, our culture, and

our whole world wants us to live in a "grey" state of mind as opposed to things being one way or the other. News media, politicians, and even some church leaders seem to push the agenda of "to each his own." My bible tells me that this is a very dangerous road and way of thinking.

Galatians 3 is very clear – It's not complicated but, it's not easy!

The bible is full of stories of rebellious people. I am a rebellious person – so are you! God wants us to choose Him! He is there! He is waiting! He will not disappoint you!

I pray that you too will use this phrase "It's not complicated, but it's not easy" as a reminder when a storm comes in your journey.

Let's not fall prey to this way of thinking that living in this "grey" area is what God has for us. God is very clear on how we should live. We make it complicated. We think we know a "better" way.

Isaiah 55:8-9 tells us that His ways and thoughts are not like ours. In Summer's bible next to this verse of scripture, she has written "Trust His plans for you!"

Summers final message to the world on this side of Heaven was a Facebook post on the morning of her accident. This message was – May Jesus be seen in me in spite of me. Thank you, Jesus for saving my little girl.

Thank you for making a way for this broken-hearted daddy when I couldn't see one. I pray I can be like Summertime in that – May Jesus be seen in me in spite of me!

It's not complicated, but it's not easy!

May God bless you on your journey.

Letter to Readers

I wanted to give the readers of this book a little history on how this book came to be. I had never set out to write a book that's for sure! I was about as lost in the wilderness of "WHY" as you can imagine!

This process was not quick nor was it easy and if I'm being totally honest I wasn't even willing at the beginning to be obedient to this yearning God had given me to tell this story. It was too hard, too painful and I was too angry. There were many times I wanted to quit!

BUT GOD…BUT GOD IS BIGGER!

He is bigger than whatever our circumstances are. I miss my sweet Summertime more than I know how to describe, BUT GOD made a way!

No matter what this world deals us He is bigger! I wanted the reader of this book to feel like they knew my precious/special daughter when they finished this book, but most importantly, I pray that when you are faced with what seems like an insurmountable circumstance or situation – whatever that may look like-that you remember GOD is bigger!

Thank you for helping me fulfill what God has put on my heart!

John 16:33 – He is Hope!

About the Author

Keith Ethridge, a Mississippi native and self-described "ordinary guy with an extraordinary story," connects with audiences on a deeply human level, sharing his journey of resilience and healing in *Forever Summer.* Drawing on his personal experience with profound grief, Ethridge offers a relatable and deeply moving account of perseverance, providing solace and understanding to those navigating loss. As a speaker, he brings this same authenticity and vulnerability to the stage, creating a powerful and engaging experience for listeners. With a background in education as a former teacher and coach, and now working in the oil and gas industry, he brings a unique and compassionate perspective to this powerful exploration of grief.

To order bulk copies of Forever Summer, or to book Keith to speak at your next event, you can contact him at: Spudjr33@yahoo.com

About the Publisher

LAKEVIEW
PUBLICATIONS

> "Everyone has a story to tell, only the courageous will find a way to get it told. Let my team and I help you become courageous!"

Helping people become courageous is something we have been doing since LakeView Publications was founded in 2018.

With every author we have helped since book one, I am reminded of the day I decided to take the big step of writing my first book. I was quickly overwhelmed with trying to figure out how to bring my dream to life, I just knew that I had a message to share with the world. If you are like I was, You are *NOT* alone! Nearly 100% of our clients started with an idea but had no idea what to do with their idea. That is where my team and I come in. We publish AMAZING books written by AMAZING people who had an idea and took a step in courage to ask the right question. The best way to start, or at least get the next steps is to ask the most important question.

How Do I Get My Book Published?

Finding the right publisher is key. The team at Lake-View Publications is driven by our passion to help people tell their stories and in helping them find a way to allow their story to take them to the next level. One of the greatest parts about assisting people in the publishing journey of their story is being able to connect with them and help them find their voice. You reach out to us with the best way to reach you, and we do the rest. It's that easy!

You wrote the book; we do everything else!

When you contact us, we will find out where you are in the process and give you an assessment of what you will need to get you from where you are to where you want to be!

Our team is absolutely magnificent, and they are dedicated to excellence. We offer proofing, editing, layout design, ghostwriting, art illustration, storyboard layout, content coaching, graphic design, and everything else you may need to get your book published and released.

www.LakeviewPublishers.com

facebook.com/LakeviewPublishing

instagram.com/lakeview_publishing

Made in the USA
Columbia, SC
02 July 2025

60253036R00054